DUNCAN MURPHY

Close Encounters

Volume 1: The Abduction Cases of Betty & Barney Hill, Travis Walton, and Antonio Villas-Boas

Copyright © Duncan Murphy, 2018

All rights reserved. No part of this publication may be reproduced, stored or transmitted in any form or by any means, electronic, mechanical, photocopying, recording, scanning, or otherwise without written permission from the publisher. It is illegal to copy this book, post it to a website, or distribute it by any other means without permission.

First edition

This book was professionally typeset on Reedsy. Find out more at reedsy.com

Contents

Foreword	iv
THE COMMON FEATURES	1
THE HILL ABDUCTIONS	12
THE TRAVIS WALTON ABDUCTION	22
THE ANTONIO VILLAS-BOAS ABDUCTION	32
THE REACTIONS	42
CONCLUSION	53

Foreword

Congratulations on purchasing *Close Encounters: Volume 1: The Abduction Cases of Betty & Barney Hill, Travis Walton, and Antonio Villas-Boas,* and thank you for doing so.

The following chapters will discuss alien abduction cases at large and these specific, famous cases in particular. It will examine the claims of the purported victims, the similarities and differences between their accounts, and the reactions to their cases from skeptics and believers alike.

Whether one believes in alien visitation to Earth or not, the following cases are as captivating as they are eerie. The idea of being taken by entities from another world, being subjected to all manner of apparent medical tests, and then being dropped off hours later with incomplete memories of what transpired has intrigued and fascinated people for decades. It is not difficult to imagine why. If these accounts and the countless ones like them are true, that means that we are not alone in the universe and there are beings visiting us who are of incalculable intelligence and posses technology far more advanced than anything that we as humans possess today.

If alien beings truly have visited Earth as so many believe, what do they want and what could we learn from them? These are the primary questions raised by the possibility of alien visitation and the following accounts suggest that these are questions we should be taking to heart.

There are plenty of books on this subject on the market, thanks again for choosing this one! Every effort was made to ensure it is full of as much useful information as possible, please enjoy!

1

THE COMMON FEATURES

There exist countless examples of accounts from people who claim to have either witnessed UFOs or to have made contact with extraterrestrial beings. While some have claimed that archaeological evidence suggests that aliens have been in contact with humanity for thousands of years, the modern phenomenon only really started in the 1950s and the 1960s. Though most believers in the existence and alien origin of Unidentified Flying Objects trace the modern belief in them to the Area 51 incident in Roswell, New Mexico in 1947, the earliest modern abduction case occurred a full decade later.

This was the 1957 case of Antonio Villas-Boas, a Brazilian man whose account will be examined later in this book. This, together with the 1961 abduction case of Barney and Betty Hill, served as the beginning of the modern phenomenon.

With so many alien abduction cases being reported worldwide, it is well worth examining just what these cases generally have in common and what the most recurring aspects of these abduction cases are.

The first common feature of close encounters of the fourth kind is, of course, the capture. This is often described as an understandably frightening event. Sometimes, the abductees say that their encounter occurred without warning, with a UFO descending on them and its occupants snatching them up. Others claim to have experienced a quite curious sensation of being compelled to travel to a specific location at a certain time. These people claim that the compulsion felt as though their very mind was being affected by some unknown force.

Some suggest that their sense of foreboding and anxiety affected them for days leading up to their capture as if on some level, they instinctively knew that they were being observed. Theorists speculate that it is possible that some aliens possess technology which allows them to alter the minds of the people that they abduct and that this could be a possible explanation for the lingering anxiety reported by some before they were taken.

The capture itself is often described as being immediately preceded by a phenomenon of sensory alteration. People describe entering an altered state of consciousness dubbed by researchers as the 'Oz Effect.' Their senses dull, they cease to perceive outside sounds and enter a state of unnatural calm, as if their brains are being affected by some unknown device.

Whether or not the abductees claim to experience this dulling sensation, what often happens just before they are taken, is the appearance of one or multiple lights in their immediate vicinity. These lights are either described as appearing from the alien spacecraft or from nothing at all. In the cases where the lights are said to seemingly have no point of source, sometimes, aliens are said to emerge from these lights directly, as if by some manner of teleportation device.

Abductees are then either led on foot by the aliens aboard their ship or levitated up by a great beam of light. Those who claim to be led on foot often describe being led through solid objects such as doors or windows, adding to the otherworldly nature of the experience. This idea of being able to phase through what appears to be solid objects adds to the idea that their technology is well beyond anything that we as humans have yet invented. Alternatively, those who claim to be levitated up by unseen forces or a beam of light often claim to have been led through an open tunnel to their eventual destination. After the initial capture and boarding of alien craft, this is often when many abductees claim to first lay eyes on the aliens themselves.

There are, generally speaking, three main types of extraterrestrials described in these accounts. The first and by far the most common is the so-called "Gray" alien. According to author and journalist, C. D. B. Bryan, in his 1995 book, *Close Encounters of the Fourth Kind: Alien Abduction, UFOs, and the Conference at M.I.T.*, some forty-three percent of abduction claims in the United States by the 1990's involved the appearance of these Grays.

Gray aliens are often described as being short, between four and five feet in height, hairless, with bulbous bald heads, large dark eyes, and the Gray-colored skin from which they get their name. Their appearance can be linked back to the earlier reports from the Roswell Incident, but in terms of their linkage to abduction cases, the first prominent case involving them was the 1961 case of the Barney and Betty Hill Abduction. The Gray alien has become iconic in terms of extraterrestrial imagery in popular culture, and both believers and skeptics alike have plenty of reason to point to in order to explain just how common this description is.

In terms of alien abduction stories involving medical procedures, the Gray aliens are by far the most common one mentioned. Some speculate that they are in fact artificial beings created by other aliens for the purpose of carrying out exploratory missions, such as the ones they apparently carry out here on Earth. Regardless of what they are, there exist so many accounts of people who have apparently been contacted by them that they have become somewhat synonymous with the term extraterrestrial. This has, in turn, caused the image to be used in a variety of television shows and movies, further reinforcing the association.

Other than the Grays, the two most common types of aliens described in encounter narratives are the Reptilian aliens and the Nordic aliens. The Reptilians can be traced back to the 1967 case of Herbert Schirmer who claimed to have been abducted by reptilian-looking humanoids. Thanks in part to the work of well-known conspiracy theorist David Icke, the concept of the reptilian alien has become far more associated with his theory that the world is secretly run by them. Due to this, far fewer people are aware of Reptillian alien abduction accounts, such as that made by Schirmer, than they are of accounts of abductions by the Gray aliens.

Nordics, on the other hand, are somewhat more common in close encounter accounts than Reptilians. They are described most often as tall beings. They are said to be fair-haired, blue-eyed, and with skin that ranges from pale to tanned. Quite notably, Antonio Villas-Boas claimed in 1957 to have encountered a blonde-haired alien. Given that his account was one of the earliest on record, it is noteworthy that the image of six to seven foot tall blonde-haired, blue-eyed humanoid aliens has not not become as culturally common as that of the

Gray aliens. Whether this is because, as the skeptics claim, the common imagery in accounts of aliens is based on previous popular sources, or it is simply that Nordic aliens are less common in their visitations to Earth than the Grays is a topic open to speculation.

Once the initial meeting with the aliens is out the way, almost every abduction case involves claims that bizarre 'medical' tests follow. Whether or not the abductee claims to have struggled against their captors, most claim to have been led to an examination room where they were thoroughly examined and tested. These tests often focus extensively on the abductee's sexual organs and reproductive system. This does occasionally include probing, thru one manner or another, but not as often as popular culture would suggest. One curious common feature in accounts of these procedures is that the alien who appears to be in charge of the proceedings is often described as being taller than his/her subordinates.

Abduction researcher Dr. John G. Miller noted in a paper he wrote in 1994 called 'Medical Procedural Differences: Alien Versus Human,' that there are often glaring differences between the medical practices of humans and those of the extraterrestrials. Whether this is due to a difference in technology or in the purpose of the examination is something that can only be speculated about.

The differences between these alien medical examinations and examinations performed by human doctors range from things like the fact that aliens are rarely described as wearing gloves to the fact that Intravenous drip is almost never mentioned. The emphasis placed by the aliens in these accounts is also curious. While their common interest in human sex organs is well known, they are rarely said to take any interest in human respiratory or cardiovascular systems. Few accounts describe them as having taken any interest in the upper torso at all. Miller also noted in his paper that he had never read one account which described the aliens as having used a 'tongue depressor.' All of this could be explained either by the aliens having access to fundamentally different technology or having very specific goals in mind for their unknown medical examinations. One other possibility, as skeptics often point out, is that in the most famous early abduction cases, the abductees were not medical doctors. Without proper knowledge of medical procedure, these abductees were therefore unable to give accurate medical descriptions of what they had experienced.

The areas of interest for the aliens in most accounts are the reproductive system, the skin, the cranium and the nervous system. The tests undertaken by the aliens often somewhat differ from account to account, but these areas of interest are almost universal.

After the initial medical exam, accounts often differ about what happens during the rest of examination. For some, that is as far as their memories go before they are returned to Earth. For others, a number of less common but still frequent, claim they are put through a form of emotional testing. This testing can take a number of different forms, with the abductees either being compelled to watch images on a screen while they are observed for their reactions, or by having the images put in their head telepathically for the same purpose. Some abductees describe being induced to interact with the hallucinations given to them. Significantly rarer is the number of claims from supposed abductees of having been instructed by the aliens to attempt to use the technology around them. In these cases, their initial confusion often gives way to an odd inherent ability to do so. Some have speculated that these accounts provide another example of alien technology, allowing them to influence the minds of humans.

One of the primary things that many abductees point out when recounting their abduction experiences, is that the aliens often communicate without moving their lips when they speak to humans. From the earliest accounts, there has been a common feature that aliens speak to one another in an incomprehensible language which involves speaking with their mouths, however, when they speak to the abductees, they seem to speak in the human's primary language but without moving their mouths. It is as though they are somehow able to communicate with humans telepathically. Whether this telepathic communication is due to some inherent mental ability that the aliens possess or due to them using some technology beyond our understanding, it is mentioned commonly enough to suggest that there may be some truth to it.

In another example of a somewhat rarer concept in abduction accounts, many abductees claim to have experienced a presentation while aboard the alien spacecraft of a child or children. The child in these claims often resembles what appears to be a hybrid between human and the alien species, often Gray aliens. Believers sometimes suggest that this is the overall goal of the aliens and the purpose of the abductions, to breed a new species of hybrid alien, a species that contains the combined DNA genetics of both the aliens and humans. If this is true, it is unknown what purpose and motivation the aliens would have in breeding a human/alien hybrid species. Some skeptics have noted that this phenomenon is a recent addition to the common features of alien abduction stories and have further traced it back to a 1991 survey done by Budd Hopkins and David Jacobs.

Some more positive accounts of alien abductions claim that following the medical exam, the aliens who are generally described as being cold and callous up to that point, suddenly become quite friendly. In these accounts, which are not truly the norm among accounts in general, the abductees are often brought to a conference of sorts wherein they discuss the abduction phenomenon with the aliens. These discussions often turn to either instructions being given by the aliens or warnings and prophecies given by them. Regardless of the form it takes, these prophecies often focus on matters which the abductees have already feared. One of the most common warnings given by aliens is with regards to the danger of nuclear weapons and the possible catastrophe of nuclear war.

These discussions with the aliens are often followed by a tour of the ship and even, in some cases, a journey through the vastness of space. People who claim to have experienced these much more positive interactions often walk away from their experiences exhibiting a degree of Theophany, or a feeling of having been close to a divinity. They can also experience a deep sensation of love either for the aliens or in general, depending on the case. Whether this and the accompanying high experienced at the moment are due to a metaphysical change in the person or Stockholm Syndrome, one can only speculate.

Regardless of how many of the common features discussed above a given abductee claims to have experienced, one feature common to all cases is the return to Earth. They are often returned to the spot that they were taken from, though this is not always the case. One common feature from most alien abduction cases is that the abductees either have incomplete memories of the events or find that they are missing their memories all together. They usually claim that experiencing lost time serves as their biggest indication that something unusual has happened. Though there are the occasional odd cases of people who find themselves missing days worth of lost time, usually, abductees find themselves unable to account for a few hours at most.

Given how often abductees are said to have been returned to the place that they were taken from, believers have often speculated that the cases where this is not done are due to simple mistakes on the part of the aliens, with Budd Hopkins having once joked that it was a "cosmic application of Murphy's Law." Such errors can mean people having been returned to a different room within the same house, or a place down the road from where they were in their last memory. One more amusing common error is the phenomenon of abductees being returned with their clothes on backward. This suggests either that the aliens felt the need to return them with haste, or that they were unfamiliar with human clothing.

For those who retain little or no memory of what transpired, they often experience what John G. Miller describes as the "realization event." This can be a singular episode or something more drawn out, but it is often a triggering of their lost memories which forces them to realize that they were victims of alien abduction. This realization can be understandably unpleasant and in some cases, it took them months after their abduction before they start to realize that something had happened to them that one, unusual day.

While plenty of abductees describe minor wounds as a result of their ordeal, often minor abrasions and occasionally marks in their skin from needles, psychological trauma is virtually as common. Post Abduction Syndrome is the term used by many believers, though naturally, it is not accepted by the medical profession. Most medical professionals remain deeply skeptical of the phenomenon of alien abduction, though there are exceptions to this rule. To deal with this trauma and often in order to restore their lost memories, abductees often turn to hypnosis.

The use of hypnosis in cases of alien abductions is controversial. Many skeptics point to the possibility for people under hypnosis to be given or develop false memories and point to this as an explanation for the entirety of alien abduction claims which they don't outright call lies. Some, however, such as Harvard Psychiatrist John E. Mack, argue against this point.

Dr. Mack points out that the vast majority of information regained by abductees who visit hypnotists is done through basic relaxation techniques, not by methods which could result in false memories. Relaxation techniques can be helpful for regaining suppressed memories because, for people who experience trauma and subconsciously suppress unpleasant memories as a consequence of that trauma, the act of holding back those memories takes subconscious effort. As Dr. Mack points out, getting these people to relax can allow them to relieve the energy involved in holding back memories and get them to come to the surface.

After getting as much of their memories back as they manage to, the abductees are then left in the position of deciding whether or not to go public. In the most famous early cases, such as those that will be discussed in this book, this resulted in an outright media circus. In the 1950s and 1960s, the idea of extraterrestrial visitations and the abduction of people were relatively new concepts and public intrigue was different than it is today. Where today pretty much everyone has heard of alien abduction and most have decided, one way or another, what it is that they believe about the topic, in the 1950s and 1960s, alien abduction was a very outlandish and frightening idea. While many will point to early evidence of supposed alien contact and even point out the similarities between cases of alien contact and cases of demonic contact from earlier centuries, the concept of alien abduction, which could hype up the mass media at the time, was quite new.

For people like Betty Hill, this meant a lifelong connection to the community which believes in alien visitation. For people such as Travis Walton, it has meant a lifetime of frequently arguing against people who claim that his account was fraudulent.

Fascination with aliens and with alien abduction has not waned in the seven decades since the Roswell incident. With fictional programs such as *The X-Files* inspiring believers around the world, the extraterrestrial phenomenon has only grown over time. With the matter of alien abduction, there are a number of key landmark cases which are often pointed to as foundational to the information that has been compiled on the topic. These cases which were so tremendously important in their time have continued to be pointed to by believers and skeptics alike to make their respective arguments on the matter. More important than the abductees likely ever realized at the time the incidents occurred, these cases have inspired others to come forward with their own accounts and have served as important moments in the history of alien abduction.

2

THE HILL ABDUCTIONS

Betty and Barney Hill were a couple in New Hampshire who, in the 1960s, claimed to have been abducted by aliens. Theirs was one of the landmark cases in the field of alien abductions, and Betty Hill herself would go on to become a well-renowned figure among those who believe in alien abduction until her death in 2004.

The pair was an interracial couple in a time when that was exceptionally rare in the United States. Barney was African-American while Betty was white. The couple lived together in Portsmouth, New Hampshire where Barney worked for the United States Postal Service, while Betty worked as a Social Worker. They were by all accounts, a pair of normal, perfectly sane people who exhibited no signs of attention seeking or mental health issues prior to their abduction.

According to the reports given by the Hills, the abduction occurred September 19th, 1961 at approximately 10:30 PM. The couple was returning to Portsmouth from a vacation in Niagara Falls and Montreal in Canada. While Barney was driving along U.S. Route 3, Betty claimed that she began to see a bright light in the distance which moved from being under the moon from her perspective to hovering in front of the west side of it. Betty, at first, assumed that she was witnessing a falling star, due to just how bright it was, but when it started to move oddly, came to wonder if it wasn't something else entirely.

As it began to move more and more unnaturally and became larger and larger, Betty urged her husband to pull over and allow them to get a closer look. Barney pulled over near a deserted picnic area just south of Twin Mountain so they could walk their dog, Delsey, and get a better look at the bizarre light. Betty looked through a pair of binoculars and saw what she described as an oddly shaped craft flying through the sky and emitting a number of different colored lights. Betty's sister had seen a UFO back in 1957, and she quickly concluded that that might possibly be what she was seeing. Barney reasoned that it was probably an aircraft on its way to Vermont, but quickly changed his mind when he noticed that it was lowering toward the ground and was growing larger. As he later recollected, he noticed that "this object that was a plane was *not* a plane."

The pair quickly returned to their car, placed the dog on the back seat, and continued on along the way to Franconia Notch, a mountain pass along the road. Curiously, the pair did say in some of their accounts that Delsey seemed perturbed through the whole ordeal, though there is no indication that the aliens cared one way or another about the canine.

They claim to have driven slowly across the narrow road to continue observing the craft and that they saw it fly above a signal tower atop Cannon Mountain. About one mile south of Indian Head, the pair claimed that the spacecraft hovered about one hundred feet above their car and covered the entire view from the windshield. Betty described it as being approximately sixty feet long and round, noting that it seemed to be constantly rotating. Barney said that it reminded him of a massive pancake.

Using their binoculars, through a window in the UFO, Barney noted between eight and eleven humanoid beings, wearing glossy black uniforms and black caps. The lead figure somehow communicated to the pair its desire for them stay still and continue looking at them. Barney, removing the binoculars from his eyes, panicked and screamed that they were going to be captured and started driving away as quickly as he could. He told Betty to keep an eye on the craft which she noted kept pace with their car with ease. As she rolled down her window to get a better look, the pair began to hear a sort of rhythmic beeping and buzzing. The sound pinged off of the trunk of their vehicle as if it was being targeted right at them.

It was at this point that the pair claims that they began to experience a sort of altered state of consciousness as their senses began to dull. They described their car beginning to vibrate and an odd tingling sensation coursing through their bodies. A second series of beeps and buzzes returned them to full consciousness. By that point, they discovered that they had traveled thirty-five miles south with only the faintest and spotty memories of how they had gotten there. As they would soon discover, it was during this bizarre trip southward that they had experienced their alien abduction.

It was just before dawn when they arrived home and they realized that their drive home had taken hours longer than it should have. They both claimed after that when they got home, they both had a number of strange impulses. Betty insisted on keeping her luggage by the back door instead of where she would have normally kept it, while Barney felt unusually compelled to examine his genitals. There were also a number of things which they could not explain about the state of their belongings as well. The leather strap on their binoculars had broken and neither could recall how. Their watches did not work and never functioned again. The toes of Barney's dress shoes were scrapped and he could not explain how. The pair took long showers in the hopes of cleaning off any remaining residue from their ordeal, though both were still not entirely clear as to what had happened.

They tried to piece together what they could remember. They both discovered that they were equally clear on what had happened up until the strange rhythmic buzzing and beeping began, but after that, all they were left with was incoherent sounds and images until they came to in their car again. When Betty dressed the next morning, putting on the clothes she had worn that evening, she noticed that her dress was torn in a number of places, as if it had been taken off by someone who either did not care to be gentle or who did not know how to remove a dress. She also noticed that there was a fine, pink powder on their clothing. The clothes have been tested numerous times over the years, but the results have never been conclusive. The final thing they noticed was the small, concentric circles on the roof of their car that looked like miniature crop circles. They had no normal explanation for how this could possibly have happened.

On September 21st, Betty contacted the Pease Air National Guard Base in New Hampshire to report the incident. The next day, Major Paul W. Henderson met with the couple and interviewed them. His report, finished on September 26th, stated that they had most likely misidentified the planet Jupiter as if that could account for anything. It was later changed to state that there was insufficient data to draw any conclusions.

Betty and Barney had not told Henderson everything about

their encounter for fear of being presumed insane, but Betty, still wanting an explanation, borrowed a book from her nearest library on UFOs written by retired Marine Corps Major Donald E. Keyhoe. Keyhoe was, at the time, the head of the National Investigations Committee On Aerial Phenomena, or NICAP, a UFO research group. Betty wrote him and informed him of their ordeal, including her description of the aliens themselves. Keyhoe passed the letter on to NICAP member and Boston based astronomer Walter N. Webb.

Webb met with Barney and Betty on October 21st that year and interviewed them for six hours. During that exchange, Barney informed Webb that he believed that he was experiencing some sort of mental block and speculated that there might be things about his ordeal that he did not want to remember. He went on to describe the craft and the entities which he stated were "somehow not human."

Webb, for his part, believed the two and chalked up the uncertainties in their accounts to normal human reactions to such incidents. Betty and Barney expressed a desire to undergo hypnosis in order to possibly help them to recover missing or blocked memories, something that Webb agreed with but did not have any expertise on.

With the thought of hypnosis put off for another time, Betty and Barney sought to continue on their lives as normal, but the memories of their ordeal continued to haunt them. Ten days after their abduction, Betty experienced starkly vivid dreams about what had happened to her during the abduction experience. These dreams continued for five straight nights and then never returned again. Despite their conclusion, she found that she could recall the dreams in great detail and stated that she never had dreams of such vividness like that at any other time in her life.

In November of 1961, she began to write down the details from these dreams. In one of her dreams, she and Barney were surrounded in their car by strange inhuman men. She dreamed that she had struggled to maintain consciousness but found that she couldn't. When the dream continued, she gained awareness only to find herself and Barney being led through a forest by the alien beings. She called out to Barney, but he seemed to be sleepwalking. The entities she described were short, between four and five feet in height, dressed in blue uniforms, with black cadet caps and with peculiar gray skin. She described them as having dark eyes, dark hair, bluish lips, and prominent noses.

In her dream, the two of them were led up a ramp into a large, round metal craft. Though she protested, they were separated, with an entity she referred to as the 'Leader', telling her that their separation would allow the process to go more quickly. She was led into a room where the leader was joined by another entity she called the 'Examiner', who had a less perfect command of English than the Leader. The Examiner communicated to her that they were going to undergo a number of tests in order to determine the differences between humans and their species.

He cut off a lock of her hair and took trimmings of her fingernails. He then examined her feet, legs, hands, throat, mouth, teeth, ears, and eyes. Using a dull knife, he scraped off loose skin cells and placed them onto what seemed like a plastic wrap, as Betty described. Finally, to test her nervous system, he inserted a needle into her navel, which caused her great pain until the Leader made the pain vanish with a simple wave of his hand.

When the tests were done, Betty spoke with the Leader and was told that she could keep a book filled with strange markings that he had given her. According to her, when she was reunited with Barney and the pair was being led back to their car, a disagreement broke out among the entities and the Leader took back the book saying that it had been decided that the pair were no longer going to even remember their meeting.

They were returned to their car where the Leader told them to wait until the craft had left so that they could watch it leave. They did so and then resumed their prior journey.

On November 21st, 1961, Betty and Barney were interviewed by NICAP members C. D. Jackson and Robert E. Hohmann. They told them of the unusual nature of their drive and how a journey back home which should have taken four hours had instead taken seven. The NICAP members said that this sort of missing time was common in UFO cases.

Within three months, the couple had begun making trips every weekend to the area in the hopes of jogging their memories or discovering clues. Though they claimed to find the spot where they were taken in 1965, they never found evidence of their abduction.

In November of 1962, the pastor of their local parish happened to invite Captain Ben W. Swett of the United States Air Force to speak there. He had written a book of poetry and in addition to reading excerpts from the book, he discussed his personal fascination with hypnosis. After the talk, the Hills spoke with him and discussed what had happened to them. Swett found the whole thing interesting, especially the matter of their missing time. He told them that hypnosis could be helpful to them, but cautioned them against going to an amateur such as himself.

By September 1963, when Captain Swett gave another lecture

on hypnosis, Barney had begun to see a therapist named Dr. Stephens. Swett suggested Barney to ask the doctor to refer him to a hypnotist. Barney did so and Dr. Stephens referred him to Benjamin Simon, a hypnotist living in Boston. Simon quickly concluded that the incident was causing Barney more anxiety than he was willing to admit. And though he himself was an outright skeptic, he came to believe that the Hills genuinely believed that they had been abducted by aliens. He told them that hypnosis could be useful for the recovery of lost memories and told them that he would be happy to help them.

Their hypnosis sessions began on January 4th, 1964, with Simon deciding to put Barney under hypnosis first. He conducted their sessions privately from one another and at the end of each one, induced amnesia to make them forget what they had discussed. This was to ensure that they could not influence one another before he was finished. It was also to ensure that they would not remember the traumatic events until he was confident that doing so would not cause them further distress.

Under hypnosis, Barney recalled first that the leather strap of their binoculars had snapped when he had run back to his car to attempt to drive away from the approaching UFO. As he was driving away, he said that he suddenly felt compelled to pull over. When he did, he was approached by six figures who told him to remain calm and to not be afraid of them. Barney narrated that the Leader told him to close his eyes. Barney reported more than once during their hypnosis sessions that it felt as though the Leader's eyes were pushing into his eyes.

His examination, as he recalled it, differed from what Betty experienced. He apparently kept his eyes closed through most of it and so had fewer details to offer. As he described it, a cup of sorts was placed over his genitals and though it did not induce orgasm, he believed that it extracted a sperm sample. The examiner seemed to count his vertebrae for some purpose and quickly inserted and then removed a thin tube into his anus. One curious detail that he gave was that the aliens, though he understood their English, seemed to communicate with him through what he referred to as 'thought transference'. Barney was unfamiliar with the word 'telepathy'.

Betty's hypnosis sessions revealed a narrative quite similar to what she had dreamed. There were some key differences, however. Most notably, the appearance of the aliens and the order of events differed somewhat. Betty and Barney's hypnosis sessions were consistent with one another and what differed from Betty's dreams differed for them both. This suggests that Betty's subconscious had perhaps filled in some missing details for her which her memories, once recovered, simply lacked. The appearance of the aliens, for instance, was said by both of them to be more in line with the now famous image of the Gray than the entities in Betty's dreams. It is possible that in her previous dreams of the abduction encounter, her mind had given the entities a slightly more human appearance while trying to fill in the gaps of her memory, simply because that was what she knew from her ordinary life.

One thing that Simon got Betty to do during one of their sessions was to draw out a star map that she described both in her dream and under hypnosis. She did so, though she stated that the stars she drew were the ones most prominent in the star map and thus most clear in her memory. According to Betty, when she asked the leader about the map, she was told that the lines between the stars represented various trade routes.

Benjamin Simon concluded that Barney's recollection was a

fantasy inspired by his wife's dreams. Barney rejected that conclusion, citing that both of their hypnotic recollections differed from Betty's previous dreams and that they had a number of details unique to themselves from the times when they had been separated from one another aboard the alien craft. He became fully convinced from the hypnosis sessions that he had in fact been abducted by aliens, and though he would never become quite as involved in the community as Betty would, he did accept that it had happened.

The couple never sought publicity for their ordeal, though they got it anyway. On October 25th, 1965, the Boston Traveller ran a front-page story entitled *"UFO Chiller: Did THEY Seize Couple?"* The reporter responsible for it, John H. Luttrell, had acquired an audio recording of a lecture that the pair had given to a small, private audience at the Quincy Center back in 1963. He also somehow managed to get his hands on notes from confidential interviews that the couple had given to UFO investigators. He found out from there that they had undergone hypnosis sessions with Benjamin Simon. The next day, the United Press International picked up the story and the Hills gained international attention as a result.

In 1966, author John G. Fuller convinced the Hills and Simon to cooperate with him and wrote the book *The Interrupted Journey* based on their experiences. It included a copy of Betty's star map. The book sold well and made their story one of the more famous early alien abduction cases.

Barney Hill died in 1969 of a cerebral hemorrhage and Betty, who died of cancer in 2004, never remarried. Betty became quite famous in the UFO community, retelling her story countless times over the decades.

3

THE TRAVIS WALTON ABDUCTION

The account of the Hills' abduction focuses heavily on the time the couple spent among the aliens, as is common for most abduction accounts. In the case of Travis Walton, his story is unique in that his time spent with the aliens often plays a very minor role in the overall account. This is due in part to how long he was missing for unlike with the Hills. Rather than being lost for merely a few hours, he was lost for a full five days without a trace. The police became involved and the media gave the case attention before he ever got a chance to publicly recall what had happened.

In 1975, Travis Walton was a forestry worker in Snowflake Arizona who disappeared at the age of twenty-two in the Apache-Sitgreaves National Forest. He worked for Mike Rogers, a man who had done contract work for nine years for the United States Forest Service. The two men were close friends and Walton was dating Rogers' sister Dana whom he would later marry. In addition to the two men, their crew included Steve Pierce, John Goulette, Allen Dallis, Ken Peterson, and Dwayne Smith.

On November 5th, 1975, Walton and the rest of the crew were contracted to work in the forest near the area of Turkey Springs to thin out the scrub brush and undergrowth in a twelve hundred acre stretch of land. Due to the scope of the project and the fact that they had been falling behind, Rogers had instructed the crew to work overtime, usually from six in the morning until sunset. Just after six in the evening on November 5th, the crew used Roger's truck to go home to Snowflake. According to the crew, just after Rogers started to drive back, they all started to see a bright light coming from behind a hill just ahead of them.

They drove on to get a better look at the odd light and from behind the hill emerged what they described as a large, silver-colored disk. According to them, it was around eight feet tall and twenty feet in diameter. Rogers stopped the truck and Walton jumped out to get a better look, running toward the odd craft. His crew-mates say that they called after him, telling him to come back, but he seemed unable to hear them. When Walton got so close and stood directly underneath the craft, the men claim that it started to move erratically, jerking from side to side and began to emit a strange noise similar to that made by a loud turbine.

At the sudden change, Walton began to back away and turned to move back toward the truck. Suddenly and without warning, a beam of light came from the craft and struck Walton. According to the rest of the crew, this beam of light came immediately after he had decided to move away from the craft. As soon as the beam struck him, it started to lift him into the air. He was apparently lifted a full foot into the air, suspended as if attached to wires, before being dropped and struck unconscious.

The rest of the crew realized that they could no nothing for their friend immediately drove off to seek help.

Around an hour and a half after they had initially finished work for the day, Ken Peterson and the rest of the crew stopped in Heber, Arizona to seek help and phoned the police. Initially, he simply told the officers that his coworker had gone missing and that he feared that something had happened to him. According to Peterson, he did so because he feared that telling them the truth would have prevented anyone from coming out, thinking that it was a hoax. Given how things would escalate, this was not an unreasonable fear on his part.

Deputy Sheriff Chuck Ellison, who took the call initially, met the crew at a nearby shopping center where they relayed them the full tale of what had happened. Two of the men were apparently in tears and all of them were visibly distressed. While Ellison found the fantastical tale to be more than a little skeptical, he did note that the men seemed genuine in their belief of what had happened. He relayed the information to his superior, Sheriff Marlin Gillespie who told him to keep the men there until he could arrive with an officer to interview them officially.

Less than an hour later, the sheriff and officer Ken Coplan arrived to speak to the men. Though they were also somewhat skeptical, Gillespie had no interest in letting a missing person's case go unsolved. Rogers insisted on returning to the area and requested tracking dogs to aid in the search. Though the department had no such dogs, officers did go along with some of the crew. John Goulette and Steve Pierce were too shaken up to be of much use, and so they elected to return to Snowflake and inform friends and family of what had happened.

When they arrived at the scene, the police quickly became

suspicious of the men and their story. There was no evidence to corroborate their claims and no sign of the missing Walton. Because it was winter and the nights in the mountainous region could be dangerously cold, officers feared that he could end up suffering hypothermia.

Rogers and Coplan left to inform Mary Walton Kellett, Walton's mother who lived on a ranch along Bear Creek, about what had happened to her son. Rogers relayed to her the story of what had happened and she replied by first asking him to repeat it and then asked calmly if anyone outside of the police and the crew had heard the story. Coplan found her calm and measured response unusual and it served to add to the growing questions that the police had about the accuracy of what they had been told. In truth, Mary Walton Kellett was a woman who, due in large part to having had to raise six children often alone, had long since gotten used to responding to bad news with calm and reason rather than hysterics. She would become more emotional and openly worried as the days went on. At three in the morning that day, she phoned her second oldest son, Duane Walton, and told him of what had happened, asking him to drive down from his home in Glendale, Arizona.

By late morning on November 6th, the police had scoured the area and found nothing to either corroborate the story that had been told to them or to lead them to where Walton was located. They grew increasingly suspicious that the abduction story had been thought up in order to cover up either an accident or a murder. On the morning of November 8, Duane Walton and Rogers entered the Sheriff's office furious because they had found no police in the area searching. By that afternoon, the police were combing the area by helicopter.

By that Saturday, news of Walton's disappearance had spread around the nation and the town of Snowflake became inundated with reporters, ufologists, and curious onlookers alike. Among the ufologists was a man named Fred Sylvanus who interviewed Mike Rogers and Duane Walton. The pair made statements which did not do them harm at that moment, but which were seized upon by skeptics for years afterward. Rogers stated that because of his friend's disappearance and the search, he would be unable to complete his contract on time and hoped that the United States Forest Service would take the unusual circumstances into consideration. Duane Walton meanwhile stated that he and Travis had been interested in UFOs for years. He added that they had both decided years ago that if they ever saw a UFO, they would get as close to it as possible and that he was confident that the aliens would not harm his brother because they simply did not do things like that.

Following this interview, Snowflake's town marshal Sanford Flake publicly claimed that the entire abduction was an elaborate prank devised by the Walton brothers involving lights and a timed release of balloons. Even Flake's wife later claimed that this was more than a little unlikely.

The police started making repeated trips to the home of Mary Walton Kellett in the hopes of obtaining more information. After Duane returned to find his mother in tears from one of these meetings, he told the police that if they wanted to speak to her again, they ought to do it at her front porch and let her go inside without complaint if it became too much for her. This was another point that would be pounced upon by the skeptics later on.

On November 10th, in response to increasing skepticism from the police to their story, the crew members agreed to take polygraph tests in order to prove that they were telling the truth. The tests were administered by Cy Gilson, an employee of the Arizona Department of Public Safety. He asked the men plainly if they had done any harm to Walton, if they knew where his body was located, and if they had in fact seen a UFO as they claimed. With the exception of Allen Dallis, whose test was unfinished, the men all passed without issue. Following this, Sheriff Gillespie stated that he believed the men's claims as fantastical as they seemed.

During this time, Duane Walton also spoke to William H. Spaulding of the organization Ground Saucer Watch, who promised him that if his brother ever came back, that GSW would arrange for a doctor to examine him. He also suggested that Duane get his brother to save his first urination in the event of his return so that it could be tested.

Late that night, Travis was returned to Earth by the aliens. As he claims, he woke on the side of a road. Looking up as he got to his feet, he saw the craft above his head and watched it leave without any fanfare. He quickly recognized the area he had been dropped off in and realized that he was along a highway some miles west of Heber. Without any alternative, he set out on foot, running as quickly as his legs would take him to the town. There wasn't a soul on the road at such a late hour or at the gas station. Using a payphone, he quickly called his sister and informed his brother-in-law of his return and his location.

His brother-in-law Grant, drove down to Snowflake to inform Duane of the call and while both Grant and Duane had doubted it had actually been Travis who had made the call, (given the media circus that had enveloped their lives, they had already received a number of prank phone calls from people claiming to be Travis) neither one felt that they could fail to follow up on it. The pair drove thirty-three miles to Heber, and much to their relief, they found Travis alive.

Upon finding Travis, Travis briefly described the aliens he met during his encounter to his brother and brother-in-law. He described them as being short and bald. Though he said their skin was white rather than Gray, he described their eyes as being large and unsettling, not unlike how Barney Hill described his abductors' eyes.

Travis was under the impression that he had been missing for an hour or so, no more than two and was horrified to learn that he had been missing for five straight days and that a massive search effort had been undertaken to find him.

Duane recalled that Spaulding had told him that GSW would find him a doctor in the case that his brother should return, and so, deciding to take up Spaulding's offer, he drove his brother to Phoenix Arizona to meet with Dr. Lester Steward. Upon meeting with him, the Walton brothers were surprised and disappointed to learn that Steward was not a medical doctor as Spaulding had indicated, but rather a hypnotherapist. The pair claims to have spent only forty-five minutes with him, though Steward would later claim that they spent over two hours with him. When Spaulding called Duane later that afternoon, Duane told him in no uncertain terms to never bother the family again, earning the man's lasting enmity.

News of Travis Walton's return reached the media and Duane received, among many other calls, a phone call from Coral Lorenzen of the Aerial Phenomena Research Organization or APRO, a UFO research group. Lorenzen promised to arrange for Travis to meet with two actual medical doctors, a general practitioner named Dr. Joseph Saults and a pediatrician named Dr. Howard Kandell. The brothers agreed and the examination began that very afternoon. Between the call from Lorenzen and the examination, the National Enquirer, a well known American tabloid, became involved. A reporter for the National Enquirer called Lorenzen and promised to finance their investigation in exchange for APRO's cooperation and access to the Walton family. Given that the Enquirer had significantly greater resources than APRO, Lorenzen accepted and the tabloid went on to complicate matters for everyone involved.

Walton's medical exam determined that he was in relatively good health all things considered, and while he did claim to have lost weight over the course of the time that he was missing, they did not notice any serious issues with him. The two things of interest that they did note were a small red spot on his right elbow that looked like something that would have been left by a hypodermic needle, and a distinct lack of ketones in his urine. If he had been without food for as long as he figured that he had, his body would have begun to break down fats to survive and the ketone levels in his urine would have risen.

In Walton's case, he did not experience quite as much memory loss as so many other abductees have reported. However, he did experience a great deal of lost time and so it is not unreasonable to speculate that Travis, like the Hills, did suffer at least some loss of recollection from his abduction experience.

Travis would later describe in great detail what he could recall from his abduction. By his description, after he was knocked unconscious by the beam of light, he came to and found himself in what appeared to be a hospital room. He was surrounded by three beings wearing orange jumpsuits, shorter than five feet tall, bald, and with large, dark eyes. His description fits the normal description of Gray aliens, but he claimed that their skin was a pallid, unnatural white instead of Gray. He said that they looked almost like large fetuses.

Upon waking, he grabbed a nearby glass cylinder and tried to break it in order to make a weapon, but it would not smash. He waved it at them anyway, and they left him alone in the room, though given how weak he says that he was at the time, it seems unlikely that this was due to fear of any sort. He left the room and made his way to a larger room with a single, high-backed chair in the middle of it. It was empty and Walton said that he felt compelled to sit in it. As he moved to do so, lights in the room turned on, growing brighter as he settled into the seat. Eventually, the lights came into focus and appeared to him as a sort of planetarium. It was as if a star map was being projected all around him. He noticed a lever next to the chair and, as he pulled it, the lights moved around him.

When he got up, the lights disappeared and he noticed for the first time, a door that he had not passed through. As he moved to open it, he heard a sound behind him and, turning around, observed what appeared to be a tall human figure. The figure was around his height, with blonde hair and abnormally large, golden eyes. The figure was wearing blue coveralls and a glass helmet. Though Walton asked the creature questions, all it did was a motion for him to follow. He did and was led into what appeared like an aircraft hangar. Three more human-like beings were there, two men and a woman. The woman moved to him and put what appeared to be an oxygen mask on his face. Although he struggled, he could not avoid it and quickly found himself asleep again, waking only when he returned to Earth.

Travis Walton underwent numerous polygraphs and hypnosis sessions over the years in order to prove that he was telling the truth and possibly regain more memories of his time with the aliens. His story would be mired with controversy more than once as he attempted to prove its veracity. Though he would fail the first polygraph he took, he would go on to question the methods of the administrator and go on to pass two more such tests later on.

He went on to marry Dana Rogers and have numerous children with her, becoming the foreman of a lumber mill in Snowflake Arizona. He published the book *The Walton Experience* in 1978, detailing his account, and it went on to sell reasonably well. In 1993, it was adapted into the film *Fire in the Sky* written by Tracy Torme, directed by Robert Lieberman, and starring D. B. Sweeney as Walton himself. It too would be a moderate success.

Though he has repeatedly defended himself from accusations of fraud over the years, accusations which have ranged from the reasonable to ludicrous, he has maintained his story for decades. He has given numerous talks on the subject of alien abduction and is believed by ufologists around the world. Today, he still lives in Arizona and still claims as he had since 1975 that for five days, he was taken and held by beings from another world.

4

THE ANTONIO VILLAS-BOAS ABDUCTION

Though all abduction accounts differ in their own ways, some more than others, few are as unique as that of Antonio Villas-Boas. Boas was a farmer in Brazil who claimed to have been abducted by aliens at the age of twenty-three on October 15th, 1957. Working on his family farm in São Francisco de Sales, Boas and other field workers had taken to working at night in order to avoid the intense heat of the day. This was not uncommon since temperatures during the day in São Francisco de Sales could become near unbearably hot.

Though the abduction itself occurred on October 15th, Boas reported that when he opened the window to let in fresh air ten days earlier, he first saw a bizarre white light coming from the night's sky. Though he thought it odd, he did not think that it was frightening until later that night when he checked to see if it was still there. He looked at it and it appeared to start speeding toward him. He slammed the shutters closed and woke his brother who also witnessed the odd light through the shutters. His brother was as mystified as he was and could not imagine where the strange light could be coming from. It disappeared after a while and did not appear again for another nine days.

October 14th, while the brothers were out in the fields working, the light appeared again. As it began hovering in the distance, Boas approached it to get a closer look. By Boas' estimation, the light hovered a good three hundred feet in the air. As he did so, it moved away from him, speeding to the other side of the field. By his account, it did this for another twenty or so times before he got bored. He could not come up with a good answer as to why the craft kept playing a bizarre game with him. As the brothers continued to watch, the odd light continued to shine and move about before vanishing, as if it had been turned off at a switch.

At one in the morning the next night, Boas was working alone on a tractor when he saw a different light appear in the sky. It was red in color instead of the brilliant white from the night before. It appeared as suddenly as it had the previous times he had seen it. The unidentified craft moved so quickly and came right toward him this time. As Boas later reported, it directly moved above him before he could even think of how to respond. The light was so bright that it drowned out his tractor's headlights. As it got closer, Boas was able to make out the source of the light, which he described as a large, egg-shaped metal craft. The craft appeared to be spinning as it hovered as if that was how it managed to maintain its flight. Three hook-shaped protrusions emerged from it, much like a landing gear of some sort. Suddenly fearful, he ran back to his tractor to try to get away from it. However, the tractor suddenly lost its power.

From behind him, a hand grabbed his shoulder. He jerked and

tried to fight off the creature. Two more joined it and together, managed to hoist him up and carry him off. He described the creatures as short, no more than five feet in height, wearing tight Gray colored uniforms which covered every inch of their bodies up to their necks. There, the uniforms were joined to round helmets which obscured their heads entirely except for their eyes. The eyes, as he described, were small and lightly colored, behind to two lenses. However, he suspected that the appearance of their eyes may have been an effect of the lenses. One curious aspect of his description is the tubes which ran from the back of their helmets to the inside of their uniform. He described them as small, smaller than that of garden hoses and colored the same as their uniform. He could not see any kind of tank or box on their back that the tubes could have connected to and he could not figure out what purpose they served.

He described their sleeves as tight-fitting and connected to five-fingered gloves. He noted that the uniforms must have been uncomfortable to move around in due to just how tight they were. The gloves appeared to restrict their abilities to move their fingers, though not enough to render them unable to grab and hold onto him. They wore distinct badges the size of a slice of pineapple made of a highly reflective metal on their chests. These badges shone with such light that at first, he thought that they emitted it, but later realized that they were reflecting the light coming from their craft.

The pants were as tight-fitting as the rest of the uniform and Boas said that he did not see a single crease anywhere in it. They connected directly to the shoes as if the whole thing was some sort of a single jumpsuit. Curiously, he described the shoes as being unusual. The soles are around three inches thick and have upturned tips. It looked like the shoes of fairies or elves from children's tales. Though it seemed that their shoes were larger than their feet, it again did not hinder their ability to move him into their ship. The only indication that the suits were as uncomfortable as they appeared was the fact that they did move quite stiffly. Despite this, they were clearly used to moving like that because they could somehow still move quickly.

Boas said that he was confident that he could have fought off one of them, given how small they appeared. However, since he was outnumbered, he was powerless to resist them.

One thing that is interesting is how much his description of the figures appeared similar to that of fairies in old folk tales. From the shoes in particular to the uneven stripes of their uniforms, their appearance, as he described them, appears to have been quite similar to the creatures from old legends. This is one aspect that skeptics have pointed to over the years when trying to dismiss Boas's account as a fantasy delusion.

Though he continued to resist as much as he could, he was pulled by the three creatures up into their craft through what he described as a flexible, metallic, rolling ladder. Once he was inside, the door closed so completely that he could not see a seam from where the metal door had parted previously. He described it as looking like a wall which never even had a door in the first place. He was led into a small square room that was entirely bereft of furniture. The room was lit by what he described as bright, square lights fixed inside the metal walls. Suddenly, a doorway opened and he was led into another room. In the center of this room was a bizarrely shaped table surrounded by backless swivel chairs which looked like barstools.

The furniture was all made of a distinctly white metal and

each piece stood on a single leg which tapered as it reached the floor. These legs were attached to the floor in different ways. The table's leg was fixed on the floor while the chairs had their legs linked to a ring in the floor in order to allow complete movement for those who sat on them.

The creatures forced him onto the table while they were communicating with one another in a distinctly inhuman language, as Boas described. He could not recognize any words of their language but they seemed to communicate through sounds similar to grunts, barks, and yelps. Boas described it as sounding particularly animalistic and unnerving. He later said that he could not replicate the sounds if he tried since human mouths and vocal cords simply could not produce them.

They stripped him naked despite his protests and he noted that they took unusual care with his clothing, as if trying not to damage it. They did not hurt him during the entire encounter, and though they were firm in getting him to do what they wanted, at no time did they become violent. After he was nude, they rubbed his whole body down with a thick, colorless, odorless, liquid substance. It was cool to the touch, but not unpleasant and it did not seem to harm him in any way. When they were done, they led him into a final room where they took blood samples from his chin and left him alone.

He was left alone in that room for what he figured was close to an hour. The room had a gray, rubber-like mattress bed where he made himself comfortable. A smoke-like substance was let into the room from holes in the wall which made Boas nauseous. He ran to one corner of the room and proceeded to throw up. When the door finally opened again, another being, looking very different from the previous beings he had encountered, walked into the room. This new being was a female. She looked human, pale, with near white blonde hair that he said looked like it had been lightened with peroxide, and she had large, slanted blue eyes. She was naked and he found her to be exceptionally beautiful. She had high, prominent cheekbones and a face which narrowed to a rather pointed chin. Her body was slim, with high, firm breasts, a narrow waist, wide hips, and large thighs. She had thin, barely visible lips and wore no makeup. Quite notably, she had bright red hair under her armpits and on her pubic mound. When Boas first told the story, he spoke only of the hair in her armpits, though some have speculated that this was due to the conservative Catholic culture that he grew up in.

Boas speculated that the clear substance that he had been rubbed with was an aphrodisiac of some sort since, despite being uncomfortable with his situation; he was suddenly consumed by a singular desire for the woman. Others have speculated that the substance was simply a germicide of some sort and that the smoke that was let into the room, which had made Boas momentarily ill, had been a chemical substance meant to allow the woman to breathe without a helmet. She would be the only being on the craft that he ever got to see without a helmet on.

Boas recalled that the woman walked right toward him in silence, staring at him deeply the entire time as if to communicate that she wanted something from him. She pressed her naked body against his, making it quite clear what she wanted from him. According to Boas, the two had a sexual encounter which lasted nearly an hour and involved a number of different acts. Throughout the entire encounter, Boas recalls that she did not kiss him, preferring to nip at his chin. Given that he had just thrown up, it is quite possible that that had something to do with it. Another possibility is a simple cultural difference between her people and humans. Through the encounter, the woman made sounds that Boas compared to growls, but never tried to speak any words to him.

When it was over, the other creatures entered the room and beckoned the woman to join them. She got up. However, before leaving, she turned to Boas, rubbed her abdomen, and gestured with her finger pointed upward. He took this to mean that the woman would return for him and take him to where she lived. He was momentarily frightened at the thought of being taken permanently from his home. In all, Boas reported that he enjoyed the encounter, but complained that he was left thinking that all they had wanted was a stallion to improve their stock.

After they had taken the woman away, the beings returned Boas his clothing and led him back to the room with the metal table and stools. They kept him there as they communicated in their odd language, ignoring him for several minutes. When they had first taken him aboard their craft he had felt fearful and uneasy in their presence, however, he recalled feeling in that moment a new sense of calm, as if he was suddenly certain that they had no interest in harming him.

He took the opportunity to get a better look at the craft itself since he had been significantly less calm than the first time he had been in the room. The walls were all made of metal and very smooth. There were no windows, nor anything which suggested any possibility of looking outside the craft.

When he noticed a small box with a glass top which appeared like a clock, he tried to take it with him to serve as a proof of his unique encounter. However, he was spotted in his attempt at thievery and the beings took it from him. As Boas described it, this 'clock' had a single hand and markings which would correspond to three, six, nine and twelve o'clock, but the hand did not move. The beings led him through more of the ship and he described in great detail the metal of the rooms that he was led through. Finally, he was led back to the ladder and the creatures signaled for him to step down. After he had descended the ladder, it retracted and the craft rose into the air. Boas watched as the landing gear retracted smoothly into the craft as well, leaving no space visible from where they might have emerged.

The craft continued to slowly rise into the air until it was about a hundred feet above his head. At this point, the lights grew brighter and a loud buzzing sound started to come from the craft. The saucer-shaped metal disk started to rotate at incredible speed and the lights started changing color until they were bright red again. With this apparent process finished, the craft shot out into the sky like a bullet and headed south. Within seconds, it was well beyond Boas' vision and was gone for good.

Boas checked checked the time on his watch. He found out that it was five-thirty in the morning, some four and half hours from when he suspected he had initially been taken. He found that his tractor had been somehow sabotaged by the craft. He did not know how they had managed to do so without touching it, or indeed, how they were so familiar with a tractor, but he found that the battery's wires had been detached.

For three or so months after his encounter, Boas reported that he suffered a number of medical issues. These included excessive fatigue, a symptom common to abduction cases as well as a number of more unusual symptoms. These included radiation poisoning, loss of appetite, nausea, pains throughout his body, headaches, a near constant burning sensation in his eyes, and an odd pattern of bruising. For the first month after his ordeal, he repeatedly developed bruises on his body which resulted in cutaneous lesions. These lesions appeared as small, red nodules which were both hard and painful to the touch. They emitted a thin, watery, yellow discharge and would be surrounded by violet-colored skin until they healed.

Dr. Olavio T. Fones, a Professor of medicine at the National School of Medicine in Brazil and a representative of APRO, convinced Boas to go public with the story of his ordeal, which he finally did on February 22nd, 1958. Boas was able to recall the details of his ordeal without the use of hypnotherapy and remains one of the few famous early abductees who did not seek out a hypnotist. Another thing which sets it apart from a number of other abduction stories is that at no point in the encounter did the aliens even attempt to communicate with him by any means other than bodily gestures and there was no attempt by them to either gain or impart information from or to him. Their purpose appeared to be entirely for reproduction.

Afterward, Boas continued to wonder about what the female being had meant when she had pointed a finger upward and had rubbed her hand over her abdomen. At the time, he had feared that it had meant that she intended come back and take him with her. Afterward, he began to wonder if perhaps she had simply meant that she would raise their child had they successfully conceived, in space and among the stars.

His story became quite popular, with the first printed version of it coming in an issue of the Brazilian UFO enthusiast periodical *SBESDV Bulletin* from April-June 1962. He himself, however, never sought nor gained true fame from his ordeal. With Brazil not having quite as much of an enthusiastic community of believers in UFOs as the United States, and with no publication on the scale of The National Enquirer picking up the story and hounding him for information, he was able to live out the rest of his life in relative peace. He became a lawyer later in life, married, and had a family. Though he never sought fame for the story, he insisted on its veracity for the rest of his life. Though he was questioned numerous times by believers and skeptics alike, he kept his story relatively unchanged with the single descriptive feature of the female alien's pubic hair being the only notable exception.

His wounds healed and he recovered from his inexplicable condition. Even the most skeptical of people who heard his story never came up with a good explanation for how a simple Brazilian farmer had ended up with radiation poisoning. With his story predating the much more famous Hill abduction by some years, one could not even say that he was inspired by other abductees.

Sources differ on whether Antonio Villas-Boas died in 1991 or 1992, but they are clear that he lived in Brazil his entire life. To his dying day, he insisted that his story was the truth and that he was abducted by the odd creatures and the even stranger woman.

5

THE REACTIONS

It is not an exaggeration to say that for the most hardcore of skeptics, no alien abduction case has ever convinced them that it is even mildly possible that there may be any truth to any such cases. These individuals generally maintain that in each case, the abduction was either an obvious hoax or that the individuals were delusional. Due to this blanket response from the critics, it is important to remember when reading about abduction cases that if the story contains a disclaimer stating that skeptics believe that the whole thing was an elaborate hoax, there is usually nothing unique about the case to make them believe it.

Skeptics such as Robert Sheaffer attest that there are usually notable similarities between the aliens and the advanced technology described by abductees and examples of such things in various science fiction novels, movies and television series. They often point out that there were science fiction programs shown on television in the 1950s and descriptions of aliens in written stories published before that. The skeptics believe that these science fiction similarities were particularly prominent with regards to the descriptions of the aliens in the Hill case and the Villas-Boas case. Skeptics believe that the Hill abduction in turn went on to inspire the common stereotypical image of the gray alien in science fiction and popular culture, which in turn influenced future accounts of alien abduction cases such as the Travis Walton incident.

Skeptics argue that abductees describe these alien beings with certain similarities, not because such beings are real and have a set appearance, but because there is a simple canon in the UFO genre which abductees usually stick to with little variation. Any actual differences in certain accounts are then explained as the creative license of the abductees themselves.

When one asks the natural question of why so many would choose to lie about such experiences, the answer is often quite simple, money. Skeptics maintain that the primary reason that people lie about being abducted by aliens is simply, 'So they can then cash in and make lots of money with book and movie deals'. When it is pointed out that most alien abductees rarely make much, if any, money from their stories, the skeptics will then say that abductees are either crazy or that they just want fame and attention. Sometimes the skeptics will even say that abductees have nefarious motives, such as a concocted scheme meant to avoid financial fallout, as is often claimed about the Travis Walton case.

The only thing that would convince the most skeptical person about these reported cases and sightings of alien abduction, would be for them to personally be abducted by these said extraterrestrial beings and experience what the previous abductees have been through. Whenever someone holds an absolute and unshakable belief about something which they have never experienced, whether it is a belief that it is based on fact or a belief that it is simply a delusion, that person holds to it faithfully. This is not to say that skepticism is necessarily a bad thing, indeed a certain amount of skepticism in life is healthy. However, simply dismissing something as being 'unscientific' without proper scientific analysis is in itself unscientific. Most importantly, it is quite worthy of a person's time to examine each case individually and determine the counterpoints in each abduction and close encounter account and then decide if they are truly based on fact or not. Then again, unless we experience a close encounter with an alien being ourselves, how can we ever truly be one-hundred percent certain either way whether these accounts are true or not?

In the case of Barney and Betty Hill, the responses were more mixed than not. As it was the first truly well-reported case of its kind in the United States, the story was met with both skepticism and awe from a population who were uncertain to what they should believe. As stated in earlier in this book, the Hill abduction story became quite popular with the UFO community and Betty Hill became a household name among them. It was so influential that even today, with so many additional cases having been recorded; it still remains one of the most popular of abduction cases within the UFO community. For skeptics, however, the tale appeared to be more than a little doubtful.

The first possibility that skeptics latched onto was the idea that the whole Hill abduction episode might well have been a shared hallucination brought about by the stress of being an interracial couple in the United States in the 1960s. The argument here was that such a thing was so uncommon and so frowned upon in certain parts that it could conceivably have resulted in psychological strain. In truth, Betty and Barney, as a couple in rural New Hampshire, never stated on record as having suffered any great inconvenience from their relationship.

Betty herself refuted the idea utterly claiming that their friends and family never had an issue with their situation and that it was never a real problem for them. Benjamin Simon, the hypnotist that they met with and a man who never believed that they were abducted by aliens, even though he believed that they believed it, stated clearly that he did not consider their interracial relationship to have been a factor.

Skeptic blogger Brian Dunning maintained that the Hill's case was questionable because so much of it hinged on the hypnosis sessions that the pair underwent. He asserted that because the hypnosis sessions occurred a full two years after the event itself, the two already had plenty of time to concoct a story together. He concluded that Betty Hill was a lifelong UFO fanatic and that the entire abduction story was her invention. This explanation failed to account for the differences between their memories recovered from the hypnosis sessions and the content of Betty's dreams or the unique features of their stories from when they were separated on the alien craft.

Even the explanation from the Air Force stating that what the couple saw in the sky was merely a weather balloon does not account for the unusual light coming from the craft as well as for the speed and quick turning ability that it seemed to exhibit.

As for the description of the aliens themselves, skeptics suggested that it came from a science fiction television series. Due to the unusual feature in their description of large eyes which wrapped slightly around their heads, researchers such as Martin Kottmeyer suggested that the most likely and possibly only source that the description would have come from, was from an episode of the science fiction series *The Outer Limits* titled "The Bellero Shield." The episode aired February 10th, 1964 when the pair was in the middle of their hypnosis sessions.

However, when asked about this, Betty Hill herself claimed to have never watched or even heard of the television show *The Outer Limits*.

Jim Macdonald, a writer from New Hampshire who lives in the area where the Hills claimed they were abducted, stated that the object the couple saw was an aircraft warning beacon on top of the Cannon Mountain. He suggested that this was a strong possibility because it is timed to light up around the time the couple claimed they first saw their UFO. The rest of their narratives he ascribed to sleep deprivation and false memories obtained under hypnosis.

Sleep deprivation and false memories became popular explanations from critics for why the couple saw and experienced what they claimed to. It is true that sleep deprivation can wreak havoc on the mind. Also, as Sheaffer claimed, the Hills were a perfect example of why driving while sleep deprived is not really recommended. Ignoring for a moment that the pair did not report having gone an extended period without sleep, it still would not account for the abduction itself and what they claimed happened.

This is where the idea that using hypnosis in these cases is often to blame for why people come to believe what they do. It is true that hypnosis can result in the implantation of false memories in people who are particularly susceptible to it. Beyond this, it is possible for people under hypnosis to have their imagination run wild and come to believe their imagined recollections to be true, when they are in fact false memories. This is why Captain Swett was so adamant that the couple should seek out the assistance of a professional hypnotist and refused to help them personally, since he considered himself as an untrained amateur and didn't want to unwittingly plant false hypnotic suggestions and memories into the Hills minds about the abduction event.

Benjamin Simon was a professional hypnotist who knew what he was doing. Even though he himself remained skeptical even after their sessions, he did not report at any point that he believed that the memories that they had obtained were false. He merely believed that the couple had come to believe what Betty had dreamed to be accurate and thus, misinterpreted whatever had actually happened to them. Moreover, the sessions were recorded and there was little evidence in these recordings that the ideas that the two had were implanted in them during these sessions.

The final prominent charge skeptics have brought against the story is that Betty, more than Barney, was a UFO fanatic. It is true that Betty's sister claimed to have seen a UFO in 1957 and that she had an interest in the idea before her own encounter. However, there is little evidence to suggest that it was more than a passing interest or that she was anywhere near obsessed before her own experience. Afterward, it is true that as late as 1977, she continued to go on UFO vigils, often multiple times a week as was reported by Shaeffer, but given what she claimed to have experienced, developing a strong interest was hardly surprising.

In the case of the Walton abduction, the accusations of the whole thing being a hoax were far more widespread and long-term. There were a number of factors which added to the skeptical response that the case received starting with the behavior of Walton's friends and family during the time that he was missing. Unlike with the case of the Hills where the greatest motive that anyone could attribute to why they would lie was the idea that they could gain fame, which is something that they didn't seek, the Travis Walton case provided skeptics with more ammunition to use in their arguments against the validity of Walton's claims.

The most common conspiracy theory with regards to the Walton case was that the whole thing was made up by Mike Rogers and Travis Walton in the hopes that they would be able to get around the terms of a contract that they were falling behind on. They had been assigned a twelve-hundred-acre region of forest undergrowth to thin out and clear away. By the time that Walton disappeared, Rogers and his crew had fallen behind on the project and it appeared that they might well not complete it on time. The theory goes then that Rogers masterminded the whole scheme in the hopes of being able to use the 'Act of God' clause in the contract to get out of it without incident. There are two major problems with this conspiracy theory and they both relate to the assumptions made by its proponents. The first, is that Mike Rogers did not activate the 'Act of God' clause nor is there any record to suggest that he ever attempted to. The second, is that suggesting that such an elaborate scheme would be preferable to having to own up to the fact that they failed to complete their contractual assignment on time. In truth, this was not the first time that Mike Rogers and his crew had run long on an contract with the United States Forest Service and yet, they continued to get jobs regardless. Undertaking such a scheme would have to be done with the knowledge that it could blow up in their faces if things went wrong. Wasting police resources is a crime, as well as fraud, which one could argue is what the whole thing would have been had it been done in an attempt to get out of a contract with the government. It doesn't seem to make sense to argue that the risks outweighed the very limited rewards.

If not Mike Rogers, then most skeptics contend that the hoax had to have been perpetrated by Travis Walton himself, if not the entire Walton family. As with the first theory, this one is aided by the unfortunate interview that Mike Rogers and Duane Walton gave while Travis was missing. Where Rogers had commented that he did not know if his crew would be able to get the job done on time while one of their crew was missing, Duane Walton's statements were significantly more consequential.

It was in that interview that Duane had stated that Travis and he had an interest in UFOs for already quite some time. They had decided that if they saw one, then they would try to get close. He was also certain that the aliens would not harm his brother. Skeptics pointed to this as evidence that the pair of brothers were already UFO fanatics and that they could have easily come up with this scheme for their own financial gain from book and movie deals. It was even suggested that Travis might have stayed at his mother's house during the five days to explain both his mother's seemingly lack of worry when she was first interviewed by the police, and her and Duane's later insistence that further talks with the police be done on her front porch.

The most damning evidence came from a polygraph examination which Travis Walton took at the insistence of the National Enquirer, not long after his ordeal. The exam was done under the agreement that the Walton brothers could veto the results if the test was done improperly and that ended up being the case. The examiner, one John J. McCarthy of the Arizona Polygraph Laboratory, did the test despite Walton's clear nervousness. The man's methods were later questioned by the Walton brothers after he determined that Travis Walton was lying. The test was suppressed at their insistence, but the knowledge of it was released anyway. Dr. David Raskin of the University of Utah later determined that McCarthy's methods were three decades out of date, but the damage was done. Even the fact that Walton went on to pass two further polygraphs did not deter the naysayers and went largely unreported.

Walton did sell a book called *The Walton Experience* based on his ordeal but has maintained that he has told the truth since the day he returned to Earth. Of the four polygraphs he has taken since that time, he has passed half, proving one way or the other that they are often imperfect tests. He exhibited no documented signs of being prone to vast lies or a willingness to seek attention at all costs. Rather, he has lived a more or less private life, free of the kind of public spectacle which came of his abduction.

Of the three cases discussed herein, the case of Antonio Villas-Boas is, perhaps the one which has been subjected to the least skepticism. There are a number of factors to this, from the incident taking place in rural Brazil, to the fact that he did not seek to monetize his story. With the story happening outside of the English-speaking world, it did not spread quite as quickly as the Hill case did. The greatest skepticism directed toward his story, however, focused not on these facts, but rather on the skeptics themselves and their supposed assumptions.

Peter Rogerson, a researcher, and UFO skeptic wrote about the story in his 1993 *Notes towards a revisionist history of abductions – Part One*, wherein he claimed that belief in Boas' story might well have come from inherent, prejudicial assumptions on the part of skeptics. In this, he asserted that the lack of skepticism toward Boas' story might have been because people simply assumed that Boas, as a lower class farmer, could never have come up with so detailed and intricate a plot. The fact that his family owned a tractor meanwhile, and that he went on to become a lawyer suggested that he was of a higher class and had received a higher education than people would have assumed and thus, as a more bourgeois individual, he was fully capable of making it up.

Though as the author of this book, I strongly feel that one could argue that classism holds no bearing on a person's ability to imagine in any way.

While fascinating, this explanation fails to account for a number of things. While it is true, as Rogerson pointed out, that an abduction story with certain similarities was published in the Brazilian periodical *O Cruzeiro* earlier in 1957, there is still no evidence that Boas ever came into contact with it. Given that this was before the height of the alien abduction craze, not as many people would have been exposed to the stories as would be the case later on. Moreover, unlike with other abduction cases, Villas-Boas walked away from his encounter with a few souvenirs for his troubles, specifically, his medical issues.

Unless that tractor was powered by uranium, there are few plausible explanations for how a farmer in rural Brazil in the 1950s managed to acquire radiation poisoning. The rest of his symptoms defied explanation as well, especially since there appears to be no evidence to suggest that anyone else suffered such medical anomalies in the area. If he had come into contact with something highly radioactive in his normal life, even if he did not notice it at the time, it is not unreasonable to suggest that he would not have been the only person in the village who had or ever did.

Without hypnosis, sleep deprivation, or monetary gain to

serve as an explanation for Antonio Villas-Boas' account, in the end, his story ends up the most believable of the three. This is not because readers would automatically assume that he was too uneducated to make it up, but because there does not appear to have been much reason for him to have done so. Even had he lied, however, it is difficult to fake such glaring and inexplicable physical symptoms as he was reported to have suffered following the incident.

6

CONCLUSION

Thanks for making it through to the end of *Close Encounters: Volume 1: The Abduction Cases of Betty & Barney Hill, Travis Walton, and Antonio Villas-Boas*. I hope it was informative and able to provide you with all of the information you wanted on the topic of their fascinating stories of alien abduction. Just because you've finished reading this book, however, does not mean that there is nothing left to learn on the topic of alien abduction.

The next step is to continue learning, not just about the other examples of abduction cases, but also on how to handle yourself in case it ever happens to you. Alien abduction is very rare. However, just because it has only ever purportedly happened to a select number of people, does not mean that it's not worth preparing for just in case. There are a number of resources available online and in print by people who have either been abductees themselves or who have simply studied the phenomenon for decades detailing how best to handle oneself in such a situation.

Cases such as the three detailed in this book are hardly alone in the history of abduction accounts. There are still other cases to read about and learn whether it's a fact, delusion or a hoax made to either gain fame or attention or gain money. Familiarizing yourself with what has happened to so many others can be helpful in assisting you with preparing a plan for what to do if you end up being an abductee yourself. Whether you do so for your own enjoyment or get ideas for what you'll do in such a scenario, the accounts of abductees can be entertaining and informative, and there is no shortage of further resources available to better inform you.

And remember, watch the skies…

CPSIA information can be obtained
at www.ICGtesting.com
Printed in the USA
LVHW042350110822
725717LV00002B/364

9 781720 067344